inspirational WORDS FOR ANY OCCASION

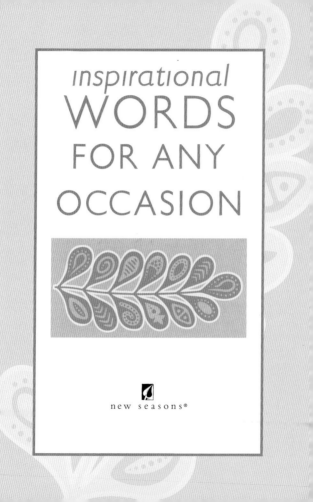

new seasons®

Original inspirations by Virginia Biles,
Emily Thornton Calvo, Marie D. Jones, Ellen F. Pill

New Seasons is a registered trademark
of Publications International, Ltd.

Louis Weber, CEO
Publications International, Ltd.
7373 North Cicero Avenue
Lincolnwood, Illinois 60712

www.pilbooks.com

Permission is never granted for commercial purposes.

Manufactured in China.

8 7 6 5 4 3 2 1

ISBN-13: 978-1-4127-9442-8
ISBN-10: 1-4127-9442-0

contents

The Right words...
Right Now

"You shall love your neighbor as yourself." Matthew 22:39

Loving our neighbors as we love ourselves is not an easy commandment. What better way to show love for our fellow men and women than to tell them how we feel?

In today's rush-rush world, we often turn to the telephone. While we are waiting in line or stuck in traffic, we pick up the omnipresent cell phone and push a few buttons and, voilà, we are talking to a friend or relative.

Or we sit down at our computers and send a group message to update everyone on our mailing list that the new baby is now one year old or that our spouse got a promotion a couple of months ago. Sometimes we engage in chat rooms with friends to find out what is happening with them.

Unfortunately, these methods of rapid communication usually do not convey a deep sense of caring or of God's love—not like committing one's self to paper.

It is a legacy of letters, not e-mails and telephone conversations, that make up our personal histories. The Victorians knew how to do it beautifully—that lovely paper filled with pen-and-ink flourishes. You can do it, too!

What's stopping you? Don't know

what to say? Don't worry. After all, it is God's love behind the words that really counts.

Inspirational Words For Any Occasion can help you know what to say. Let us help you get started by suggesting phrases that are appropriate for the occasion. Then you can do it!

Keep it simple! Keep it from the heart! Keep in touch!

birthday wishes

A birthday marks another year of God's love. When you want to celebrate someone's birthday, pick up a pen and tell him how much God loves him. The perfect words will make anyone's birthday even more of a cause for celebration.

• God loves you, and so do your friends. Enjoy all the love and affection that come your way today. Happy birthday!

• God is smiling on your special day. Happy birthday!

• A birthday is a day for reflection: a day to celebrate you as a child of God, made in his image.

• May laughter, contentment, and God's love decorate your day and fill your year. Happy birthday!

• The secret of a happy life is to *"do justice, and to love kindness, and to walk humbly with your God."* Micah 6:8 You have discovered that secret! Have a wonderful birthday!

• May God's love surround you on your special day.

• May the joy you give to others come back to you on this day.

• You touch everyone you meet with your generosity and love. Use this special day to treat yourself with the same goodness! Best wishes on your birthday.

• This is God's day, and you are God's child. Have a wonderful birthday!

• Wishing for you a day that holds all of the blessings God can bestow. Happy birthday!

• The simplest treasures are God's gifts. May you delight in God's gift of life on your birthday!

• Hoping your day is a pearl to hold close. Happy birthday!

• Savor each day for God's gift that it is.

• May your birthday make you feel as loved and as special in God's eyes as you are!

• God has given you exactly 86,400 seconds in your birthday. I pray you enjoy every one of them!

• Methuselah lived for 969 years, but the importance of birthdays is not how many years you've had—rather, how well you have lived them. Best wishes for many more!

• May angel wings hover about you on your special day!

• Your life shines with all the colors of the rainbow. Keep painting!
Happy birthday!

• *"Gray hair is a crown of glory; it is gained in a righteous life."* Proverbs 16:31
This says it all! Happy birthday!

• Another birthday, another year of recollections of God's love.
Let's celebrate!

congratulations!

One's success is due to God's grace.
While you are congratulating the
happy recipient, remember to share
the honors with God.

• God has given you great joy, and your joy has brightened my life, too. Congratulations!

• When the Lord is with you, you will have great success in your undertakings. Congratulations!

• *"The human mind plans the way, but the Lord directs the steps."* Proverbs 16:9
Whatever you and the Lord have been doing, keep doing it! Congratulations!

• You are proof that dreams and possibilities are endless when you walk in God's path. Congratulations!

• You have walked in the footsteps of the Lord. Enjoy the love, laughter, and success that are yours today.

• I hope this is the first of many blessings to come. Congratulations!

• *"For to the one who pleases him, God gives wisdom and knowledge and joy."*

Ecclesiastes 2:26

Thank you for letting me share your joy!

• The heavenly choir is singing a song in your praise. Congratulations!

• The Lord has weighed your spirit and found you deserving of the best. I am so happy for you!

• The Lord has rewarded you for a job well done! It couldn't have happened to a nicer person, and I am overjoyed for you.

• You have committed your work to the Lord. No one deserves success more than you do. Congratulations!

• *"Wisdom is a fountain of life to one who has it."* Proverbs 16:22

You are so blessed! You have it all!

• My heart joins with yours in singing praises to the Lord, who has given you such a wonderful gift

• Praise God for the happiness you are feeling today. May it go on and on and on!

• *"Well done…Because you have been trustworthy in a very small thing, take charge of ten cities."* Luke 19:17
You have done well, and God has richly rewarded you. Congratulations!

• *"Your young men shall see visions, and your old men shall dream dreams."* Acts 2:17
Dreaming a dream is easy; following that vision is not! Congratulations on your achievement!

• A new job will bring you new challenges, but I know you can handle it. Congratulations and God bless!

• You have been God's good and faithful servant, and you deserve this success!

• I am so proud of you and your accomplishments. I hope this is the first of many great things to come!

• This is a wonderful day for you. You have walked in the steps of the Lord, and he has led you to success.

• Luck has nothing to do with your success. You and God made it happen! Congratulations!

• *"But let all who take refuge in you rejoice; let them ever sing for joy."* Psalm 5:11

I have heard your good news, and I rejoice with you. Congratulations!

• God brings good things to good people—and you deserve it!

saying thanks

If we remember that our gifts ultimately come from God, our gratitude will be easy to express. Pick up your pen and tell someone how their loving kindness made you feel.

• You have let your light shine in so many ways. Thank you for all you have done for me.

• My "thank you" seems so small compared to all you've done, but it comes from my heart.

• Every single thing you do reflects your caring spirit. Thank you.

• Only you could have known exactly what would make my day. Thank you for knowing me better than I know myself.

• God's gifts to us are wondrous! Your gift to me is wonderful! Thank you for being so thoughtful.

• God bless you for your concern. You help me put my life into perspective.

• Sometimes simple words say it best: Thank you!

• Kind deeds like yours change lives. Thank you.

• God has given us countless gifts of love. You are special to me.
Thank you.

• Your love and faith have comforted me. Thank you for being there for me.

• Your kindness reflects your love of Christ. I'll always remember your loving actions.

• Generosity is a sign of a great soul and you're surely one.
Thank you for everything.

• You've restored my faith. I'll be forever thankful.

• I'll always be grateful for your love and caring. Thank you.

• You are truly God's child! Your kindness will be remembered. Thank you.

• *"God our maker doth provide."*
Thanksgiving hymn
Thank you for your generosity.

• May life bring you a reflection of the kindness you've shown to others. Thank you for your thoughtfulness.

sympathy

When sad or terrible events happen
to people you love, your caring words
from a loving heart can make a
difference. Remind those who hurt
that God loves them.

• When your heart is empty, filling it with happy memories can help you through the dark hours. Remember that God is with you.

• It is hard to understand why those we love are taken from us, but find comfort in knowing that he/she rests in the arms of Jesus.

• May your faith carry you through this sorrowful time.

• Take heart. God never gives us more pain than we can bear.

• Always know you're never alone. Jesus is by your side even when you can't see him.

• My heart aches for you. I'm sorry for your loss. Put your trust in God, and put your heart in his hands.

• **Jesus said,** *"I tell you, you will weep and mourn, but the world will rejoice; you will have pain, but your pain will turn to joy."*

John 16:20

Remember that life will be better again.

• When the Lord calls our loved ones home, he leaves a gift of memories in exchange. I'm here if you want to talk.

• It takes a little darkness for us to see the stars, and a whole lifetime to reach them. Don't give up.

• Memories are the legacy of God's love.

• Talking to God will help ease the pain. I am also here to listen and grieve with you.

• Jesus is helping you carry your burden, but I'd like to help also.

• God is always in your corner at a time like this—so am I.

• After so many years together, you have a wealth of memories to embrace and again feel his/her presence.

• I was shocked to hear of your loss. I will keep you in my thoughts and prayers.

• My arms are not long enough to reach across the miles to you, but God's arms are. I am so sorry for your loss.

• You are in my thoughts and prayers every step of the way.

• Open your heart to the warmth of family and friends. Open your soul to the prayers of those who care. You are loved so very much.

• God is with you in your sorrow as he was with you in your joy. May your faith bring you comfort.

words of comfort

When friends or loved ones face
troubles or suffer pain, they need
support and encouragement. Yet it is
often hard to find the words to
comfort them. Use the following
caring phrases and suitable words
to show them your love.

• May this setback bring a life that is richer than before.

• No one can truly understand how difficult this time is for you, but you have our love and prayers.

• No matter how heavy the burden, God will be there to share the load you carry.

• When problems on the job seem too much to deal with, remember that you are bigger than your job and stronger than your problems.

• I pray that the fog of this depression soon lifts, revealing clear, blue skies again.

• Believe in tomorrow, and let faith guide you through today.

• You worked hard and came a long way. Don't worry; you'll do it again.

• May God give you the strength and the courage to deal with the misfortune that has befallen you.

• Don't fret. You're sure to find the person who is right for you.

• It's not failure—only change,
awakening, and the opportunity
for something positive to bloom.

• May God's love fill you with hope,
healing, and the forgiveness needed
to resolve the personal struggles you
are dealing with.

• Love isn't gone forever. It's merely
waiting in the wings for the time when
you are ready once again.

• Forgive. It's God's way. Let it also
be yours.

• With God's help, you'll find the path you need.

• Pray for guidance, and God will help you mend this relationship.

• Alone, we stumble headlong into the night, but with God's grace we walk in loving light.

• When there is healing to do, call on God's wisdom, guidance, and love.

• I pray that God's love will be the soothing balm you need to heal the wounds of your divorce.

• I heard about your situation, and I'm so sorry this had to happen. I have everyone I know praying for you!

• God will be there in your darkest hours to walk with you. You are not alone.

wedding Bells

A wedding is one of life's most joyful
events. Jesus' first miracle was at the
wedding feast in Cana, and we are
reminded of his loving and caring.
Be sure to include him in your note
of congratulations.

• May God grant that the joy of this day be yours for the rest of your lives together.

• May God bless your love so that it continues to grow stronger with each passing day.

• Today is a day you'll remember forever. Treasure it, as God treasures you both.

• God has joined your hearts. Let him lead the way through your life together.

- Health. Wealth. Happiness. May your life together be abundantly blessed.

- May the light of love cast its glow on your lives from here to eternity. Love and best wishes.

- Two people. One life. One love. Blessed by God from this day forward.

- *"A time to love…"*   Ecclesiastes 3:8
May the love you share today grow stronger every day of your lives.

- May your love and happiness always reflect God's gifts to you.

• I believe the sound of wedding bells rings all the way to heaven! Have a wonderful wedding day.

• May the exhilaration of new love remain in your hearts through eternity.

• God has chosen you for each other. Congratulations and best wishes.

• God's love is unfailing; so must your love be for each other!

• God has smiled on your love and happiness!

- Let God, and love, lead the way in your life together.

- Today you make the most important promise you will ever make.
God bless.

- Cherish each other every day, and you will experience a lifetime of love and happiness.

- You two deserve all the love and happiness in the world.

- One life is a miracle, but two lives knit together is a joy beyond words.

• God knows you're perfect for each other... and so do I!

• Enjoy love and good times from this day forward. You are blessed because God has smiled on your union.

• Yours is a marriage made in heaven.

• I hope the two of you will always share the caring, closeness, and faith you share today.

Thinking of you

What a thrill to receive a note in the mail from a friend! How much better it is to send one! Just be sure to tell your friends that they are missed and that they are in your thoughts and prayers.

• *"See what love the Father has given us, that we should be called children of God."*   1 John 3:1

You are my friend and my thoughts are with you.

• *"Let us love one another."*   John 14:7

I love you as a friend and a child of God. I miss you!

• If absence makes the heart grow fonder, you must be my fondest friend. Please keep in touch by letter and prayer.

• Out of sight, out of mind? Not a chance! I cherish the hours we've spent together.

• *"Since God loved us so much, we also ought to love one another."* 1 John 4:11

We may be far apart, but you're always in my thoughts.

• Although our lives have taken us miles apart, there is no distance between our hearts.

• Just because you haven't heard from me lately doesn't mean you haven't been in my thoughts and prayers.

• "Wish you were here" just doesn't express how much I miss you. I pray for the day God brings us together again.

• I've been thinking about you so much that I feel like we're together again. May God's love be with you until we meet again.

• Just the thought of you makes me feel closer to home. The earth will sing for joy when we are together again.

• When you're not with me, I am not whole. You are the miracle that makes my life complete.

• May God bless you! I miss seeing your smiling face and pray that all is well with you.

• Just thinking of you can make me smile and feel happy. You are a blessing to me even when we can't be together.

• Time has a way of slipping away— let's hold tight to our friendship.

• I just want to reach out and tell you how much I miss you. God be with you until we meet again.

• When I think of your laughter, I hear the tinkling of angel music, but still I miss you.

• I wish I could reach out and hug you. Since I can't,

"The blessings of the Lord be upon you."

Psalm 129:8

• If God would grant my desire, you'd be here with me now.

• Hold God's love in your heart, and you'll never feel alone.

get well soon

A simple note will let loved ones know that God cares about them. Your expression of love and caring will ease the road to recovery.

• May God grant you a speedy recovery.

• Get better soon—there is still much joy ahead of you!

• While your body regains strength, let my love and faith help sustain your spirit.

• I'm sorry you've been under the weather. You are in my thoughts and prayers.

• The angels bring you wishes for a speedy recovery!

• May God's healing touch be upon you. May God's loving spirit be within you.

• Best wishes as you fight this illness. My prayers are with you.

• Don't hesitate to call on me if you need anything. I'd be honored and blessed to help!

• Prayer can be a powerful healer. Place yourself in God's hands.

You're a great friend

Friends are the greatest of God's gifts.
John cautions us to love our friends
and treat them as children of God.
Take time to tell your friend what he
means to you!

• A friend is a guardian angel in disguise. Thanks for always watching out for me.

• *"Let us love one another."* 1 John 4:7
You're like family to me. Thanks for being such a great friend.

• Thank you for being you—the greatest friend I could ever have.

• When I count my blessings, our friendship tops the list.

• We know so much about each other. I am so grateful to have you in my life.

• God has given you to me as a friend. I thank him every day.

• To have one true friend is lucky. To have a friend like you is a blessing.

• You are my angel on earth! You touch my life in a million wonderful ways.

• Good friends are the rare jewels of life — difficult to find and impossible to replace. I thank God for you!

I LOVE YOU

Love between a man and a woman is truly blessed by God. Let your loved one know how much you care by saying the right words!

• You make my life complete.
I love you.

• My heart beats because of you.
My life is you. I am surely blessed.

• Our relationship is a blessing. Please
know that I love you.

• God gave us to each other to have
and to hold forever.

• Your love is my most treasured gift.
I thank God every day.

• I will love you through eternity.

• Love is God's greatest gift. Without your love, I wouldn't be the person I am today.

• *"Your love is better than wine."*
Song of Solomon 1:2

Indeed your love is like life to me!

• The angels are singing our song! I love you.

• I thank God every day for the gift of you.

• I found love, laughter, and life when I found you. I treasure you.

• My life with you is better than I ever imagined it could be. Thank you for your love and companionship.

• Love shared is love multiplied. I want you to know I love you.

• Anywhere with you is where I want to be.

• *"My beloved is mine, and I am his."*
                              Song of Solomon 2:16

I thank God that we belong to each other.

Happy
Anniversary

Anniversaries—your own or someone else's—remind us to count our blessings. Bring a smile to someone's face by reminding her how much God loves her.

• May every tomorrow be twice as sunny and sweet as all the days that have passed. I thank God for each day.

• May God bless you as you continue to grow together in life and love.

• Congratulations on your golden anniversary. Fifty years of wedded bliss, each worth its weight in gold.

• *"Set me as a seal upon your heart, as a seal upon your arm; for love is strong as death."*
Song of Solomon 8:6

I love you more with every year we share.

• *"Many waters cannot quench love, neither can floods drown it."* Song of Solomon 8:7
My love for you grows stronger with each passing year.

• Celebrate the special love that God has given you.

• The best way to enjoy life is to savor the passing of time. Let's celebrate another year together and thank God for his blessings.

• God has given us everything we need, including each other. Let's cherish his gifts.

• *"Enjoy life with the wife whom you love, all the days of your vain life that are given to you under the sun."* Ecclesiastes 9:9

Let us follow God's wisdom and love each other forever. Happy anniversary.

• Your love is an inspiration and example of what God intended love to be.

New Baby

There's no greater miracle than the birth of a new baby. Rejoice with the new parents about the gift of God's great love.

• God has blessed you with the greatest miracle. May the joy of parenting bring you a lifetime of laughter and love.

• The miracle of life reveals itself in the tiny expressions of a newborn child. Congratulations on your miracle.

• May your new little angel open your eyes to all that is beautiful in life!

• What could be nicer than a brand-new baby to love. We praise God for his blessing!

• God has blessed you with a sweet little bundle of love.

• Congratulations! Heaven has smiled on you!

• May you and your baby feel God's love always.

• A baby is life's greatest blessing. Congratulations!

• Look at this!
A brand-new reason to smile!

Happy Holidays

Christmas is indeed a time of celebration! Put Jesus at the center of your traditions as you reach out to loved ones.

- May God bless you and keep you, now and throughout the year.

- May the peace, joy, and love of Christmas be with you throughout the year.

- Wishing you God's love during this holy time!

- 'Tis the season to remember God's wonderful gift to the world.

- May the joy of that first Christmas be with you now and always.

• God grant you a blessed Christmas, filled with peace and contentment.

• May you be granted the richest blessings at Christmas and throughout the year.

• May the miracle of Christmas fill your heart with joy.

• I wish you peace this holiday season, and I hope you are guided by the strength of the Lord in the coming year.

Graduation

Graduation is truly the first day of the rest of one's life—a life that is full of the promise that God has made. When you write a note of congratulations and best wishes, focus on this promise of God.

• God grant that all paths lead to happiness. May all of your hopes and dreams come true!

• Wishing you success on your graduation and always. God be with you on your journey through life.

• For all the successes behind you, I send my congratulations. For all the challenges ahead of you, I send my blessings.

• Congratulations! What a blessed achievement!

• Hold tight to the dreams you have today and walk with God in their direction.

• God has blessed you with wisdom and courage. Follow your dreams! Have a great graduation day!

• Congratulations on your graduation! Always be proud of your achievements, and use them to fulfill the promise of the life that God has given you.

• Graduation is just one day, but it reaps rewards to last a lifetime.

• We are so proud of your accomplishments—in the past, and especially today. The heavens are smiling on you!

• Wishing you adventure, success, and happiness for all your tomorrows.

• Look boldly into the future and be confident as you walk your life's path.